How To Turn Your Woman into A Raving Nymphomaniac

For Men Only

By
Mike Riley

ISBN# 978-0-9895532-2-3

Published, printed and bound
by Mike Riley
Aboard the Beau Soleil somewhere on the Seven Seas

And
For sale by Amazon and Kindle

http://www.amazon.com/author/mike.riley

sailingbooks@rocketmail.com

No Animals or Women were Harmed in the Writing of this Book

Table of Contents

Preface

Women are the most beautiful and fabulous part of life on Earth. Life wouldn't be worth living if it wasn't for the girls. Too bad they are flawed. Not that it is their fault. It isn't. They start out perfect; their parents, their teachers and civilization's morals, destroy them.

They are taught that they should never touch themselves down there. That their private parts are dirty. They are told that girls who make themselves feel good that way are going to hell, will never get married and they would never have any friends.

By the time we fall in love with them they are racked with guilt and frustration. Some can conquer their past and live a happy life but they are few indeed. The rest are taught that it is their duty to have their husband's children but it is going to hurt like hell. Some are even taught that everything hurts down there. No wonder parents, clergy and governments don't want us to have pre-marital sex. If we found out how screwed up our prospective mates were, we might run like hell to get away from them.

We didn't know that after marriage, love would be interspersed with tears and weeping, that men were condemned for wanting to do anything but the missionary position, that our desire that our mates should enjoy sex as much as we do, would be considered cruel and unreasonable punishment.

Many men live their lives thinking this it is just the way it is. As their desire to please their woman fades, so does some of their love. Soon, they are leaving separate lives; marriage, children gone, becomes just a convenient way to reduce taxes.

There has to be a better way. Why can't we wake our wives and/or sweethearts up? Break them loose from their childhood programming? Reach out to them and turn them into our equal sexual partners? Equal? No. Turn them in to raving sexual creatures that attack us when we enter the door! Who can't wait to get their hands on us! Who want to use our bodies for their own pleasure!

It can be done. This book shows the way. Happiness is in your future and you can have joyful, incredible sexual pleasure with the girl of your dreams! Just wake her up! Wake her up so that she realizes and becomes the sensual, sexual woman that she was born to be!

Women speak a different language than men. They really do! Some cultures recognize this and men and women really do speak different languages. They have lawyers who are versed in each sexes' languages to solve problems! In reality, all men and women speak differently. Men speak with logic and facts, women speak with emotion and feelings. To be able to influence your girl to embrace her sexuality, you are going to have to learn at least some of her language. Oh, stop it. Relax. You won't turn into a sissy or become gay. But you will find yourself with one hot girl!

Women think about sex differently. They don't like porn. Women really don't. Men do. Men like to think about sex visually. Like in how sexy their girlfriend's body is, look at the centerfold in Play Boy or like: where is the clitoris anyway? Who has a picture? Women think about sex in words. They don't look at porn, they read romance novels. *(Have you ever read one of those things, guys? They are hot!)* Women like to talk things out. Guys like to draw plans and fix things preferably without the directions.

Most of all, men have different hormones racing around their blood streams than women do. Well, actually, they have the same hormones but in far different concentrations. It is these hormones working with and against each other that make men and women so different. Babies all start out as female. Hormones make some turn into males. Hormones, directed by the brain, make some women have little desire for sex, while others they make into nymphomaniacs. Hormones can make women want to get it on everyday they can. You can change your girl's hormones. You can turn your girl into a sex goddess!

Read on, soon to be satiated with happiness, male!

How Women Work

Imagine you live in a world with boring cooks. Everything is cooked the same way, every time. Spices are not allowed. No fast food, no alcoholic drinks, no soda; this imaginary world is great for vegans except there is only one variety of apple for the only fruit and the only vegetables are carrots.

This is the sexual world most women live in. It is the world they were taught to live in. Anything unusual is sinful, forbidden, a one way ticket to someplace even worse. *(What could be worse?)*

The only way we can live happily with these girls is to open up their eyes, to show them this wonderful world we live in, to share with them their God given bodies with all their interesting curves and promontories. We have to develop their appetites for the many different ways of making love. When a person first tastes a new food, she doesn't always like it. Over time however, hopefully, she will discover the pleasurable nuances of the new experience.

It won't be easy. We are fighting against decades of programming. But we have an ace in the hole. Sex really feels good. I know it feels good to us men, but it really feels good to women! Researchers agree that when a women orgasms, at least 100 times the number of nerves resonate in their bodies as men. The potential for intense sexual desire is inside every woman. Really! If you are laying there in bed with a wife that tells you repeatedly, "Not tonight, Hon, I have a head ache." You might not believe me. But it is true.

Did you ever try to finger a girl when she was driving a car? You can't do it. She loses control. Her eyes unfocus, she loses fine motor control of her legs, her brain stops thinking about the future, about that stop sign down the road. She can give us a hand job while we are driving, no problem. We still retain control of our brains and our nerves. Women can't. Women have very intense orgasms. Lucky creatures!

It has to be this way or why else would they ever have a baby twice? Once to learn her mistake and for the experience, sure. But then, she would swear off sex for life. Maybe that is why their brains turn off while making love!

Women really like sex. Often they like it so much that it scares them. Being out of control is very scary. The idea that any man in the know can turn them into a mindless sex machines is exceptionally scary. It makes them very defensive. If any man is going to turn her on, it better be Mr. Right. Someone who will take care of her, respect her, adore her and appreciate her. If she is going to be helpless when a guy touches her, it damn well better be some guy that deserves her. Hey, you can't blame women! If we men were in the same spot, we would react the same way. Or actually, maybe not!

Women are just like men only more complicated! They are! Really! It isn't like I am telling you something new. Everyone knows that women are complicated. Ask them how they want their steak cooked and they start crying and jabbering away about how you never talk to them anymore. Complicated, right? Absolutely.

No one understands women, except maybe other women. But just try to ask your wife's girl friend what is wrong with your honey and she will look at you like a bug that just crawled out from under a rock. You know why? It is because the girl friend doesn't understand either but there is no way in hell she is going to admit it! They are sisters and you are the enemy; the guy that made her cry.

Girls have an intense inner life. They learned to keep things internalized early in life when their mother loaded guilt on her if she didn't obey. Guys had it easy. Our fathers told us to do it their way or we would get punched. After a few experiences, we still did what we wanted but learned to keep out of his way. No guilt involved. Lucky men.

When we asked our girl how they would like her steak cooked, the dam of their inner feelings broke open and the flood started. Like all floods, a little excess water quickly builds into a disaster. First the tears, then no dinner and a cold bed. The next morning she is threatening to move back with her mother, all because you asked her how she would like her steak cooked? What is going on? Sure, you love her, but she really makes it hard. Why couldn't she have just said medium rare?

What is happening is she is royally frustrated. Sexually. I know. I know. She makes little noises of satisfaction when you are making love. News Flash. She is faking it. Really. She is faking it to get you turned on so you finish quicker and she can get some sleep. Sad but true. Answer me this. After you make love to her and then call out her name, poke her in the arm, sprinkle water in her face, does she react? If she does, she was faking it. Us men have no idea how intense a female orgasm is. Remember in science class when they showed us the little pea that was the Earth and the huge beach ball that was the sun; the Earth is our orgasm, the whole solar system is hers. Bummer, huh? But why else would she have more than one child? Really! We can only imagine the pain. Unfortunately, if your wife ever did have a true orgasm, it was so far in the past that she has half forgotten about it. No wonder she is frustrated! Dreams are always better than reality. *(Don't worry, by the time you finish reading this book, your girl will think she has gone to heaven with the guy who woke her up, who gives her multiple orgasms every night!)*

Women's emotions are ruled by hormones. What? You didn't know that? Really? There are over 600 hormones racing around a woman's body. No wonder they are emotionally complicated! Imagine having 600 bosses telling you what to do all the time, 24/7! But stop complaining. This is a good thing in a way. Because she has so many emotions ruling her and because they change so easily, it means that we can change her emotions to the ones we like, if we only know how. Guess what? This book tells you how! This book tells you how to turn your woman on to the emotion that makes her into a raving nymphomaniac! A part of every woman, no matter how chaste she may act, is a desire to be taken over and over again. Every single woman alive has this emotion somewhere inside her. All you have to do is learn how to bring out that emotion to rule her body, at least for some of the time, at least one night a month, if not at least three times a week! *(Every night if we are still under 60!)* We can do that by changing her hormones. Which hormones? Fasten your seat belt! Here we go!

Sexually, the hormone that makes the most difference is oxytocin. This hormone enlarges and moisturizes the vagina, causes the clitoris to become sensitized, causes the nipples to grow longer and the areoles to crinkle up and activate the nerve that leads from them directly to the clitoris. Oxytocin is the female love hormone. Memorize this one, Oxytocin is your friend!

Oxytocin is one of the most unusual hormones ever created. God had a good day when he invented it. *(If you are a Creationist.)* Other substances humans take to influence their behavior, alcohol, tobacco, caffeine, cocaine, heroin and other drugs need greater and greater quantities to obtain the same affect. Not oxytocin. The more you love, like, grok, desire, the more you give, the more you receive graciously, the more you can and the more powerfully this hormone affects us. Each of the above things releases oxytocin into the blood stream. Oxytocin makes us love, makes us human. Oxytocin is the hormone that gives us our humanism.

(Oxytocin still resists all attempts to artificially fabricate it. Mostly because swallowed as a pill or injected into the blood or sprayed into the nose creates extreme side effects like: hemorrhage in the brain and uterus, increased blood pressure, heart rate and cardiac output, all deadly.)

Every hormone has its anti-hormone. Another hormone that migrates its affects or deletes its influence. Cortisol is lessened by oxytocin. Cortisol makes us jittery, nervous, anxious and sinks us into depression. Oxytocin not only prevents all of that but reverses many of the diseases caused by Cortisol: impotence, depression, addiction, some cancers, plaque in the arteries leading to the sexual organs *(both sexes)*, increases bone density while low levels of oxytocin leads to osteoporosis.

As cortisol goes up, oxytocin goes down and visa versa. Before Freud convinced the world that psychotherapy was the way to heal over stressed women, the normal practice to help women was 'medical massage', or giving the poor girl an orgasm. This worked very well as orgasms release oxytocin which lowers cortisol which causes stress.

Testosterone is the male sex hormone that makes the man's penis grow larger and balls tighten up. Women produce testosterone also. In women testosterone increases her sex drive and increases the size of her clitoris. Higher amounts of this hormone also increases her aggressiveness in bed and causes her to grow a little fuzzy facial hair. Her body, laced with testosterone will demand sex more often, very often repeatedly. Testosterone in women is good. So what if she has a little mustache? Who cares? Razors are cheap. Sex isn't. How great if your girl takes you out to dinner, wines and dines you, all to get into your pants! Any girl can increase the supply of testosterone in her blood stream. *(Read on if you want to find out how you can do it!)*

Despite what Yul Brenner said in the original movie 'The King and I', women are the bees and men are the flowers. Women are designed to go from man to man, not men from woman to woman. It is true! *(Sorry, I know you didn't want to here that.)*

Humans have spent the vast majority of their time here on Earth living in caves, at least they did if you believe in Darwin's Evolution theories. Early ancestors of humans came down from the trees and started walking upright between 5.3 and 1.6 million years ago. *(It took a while to give up swinging from trees and eating fruit whenever you wanted. Apes were the original Hippies!)* Cro-Magnon *(more or less, us)* developed 30,000 years ago. They were the cave men that Hollywood likes to show in their movies. *(There were many other proto humans that died out.)* About 7,000 years ago towns and villages started to form. So depending on where you draw the line, we as a species lived in caves for 20,000+ years. Long enough to create some habits! Long enough for those habits to be part of our hormonal life. When a couple make love, the man falls asleep after they have climaxed. Not the women. She is wide awake after an orgasm. Women are capable of many, many almost continuous orgasms. *(Actually about 5 minutes apart.)* How could this possibly have developed? There can only be one answer. The women after climaxing with one man, moved on to another and another and another. Her baby would be the result of the very best seed! Instead of the strongest of your sperm fighting to go upstream, it was the strongest of all the sperm in the cave trying to be the first to the egg! Women were designed to make love all night long especially in the middle of their cycle. *(More on that later!)* Women are all, genetically, historically, nymphomaniacs! And they still are today. Us men just have to wake them up!

Don't think your woman is going to be sleeping around with all your friends. She isn't living in a cave any more. But she still retains the desire to orgasm more than once a day. All women do. It is the big hidden secret of sex. Very often, women give up on sex because, for them, it just isn't worth it. For a woman, to orgasm only once is like for a guy to almost get there but not to ejaculate. Bear in mind that when you turn your girl into a nymphomaniac, you are going to have to satisfy her, over and over again! Every day! Before you start messing around with a perfectly good female, make sure you can handle the new her. Maybe you should start eating oysters! If you could speak Female, you would know that when your girl is crying about how you never talk with her when you asked her how she would like her steak cooked, she is really saying, 'I am as horny as hell and you aren't doing anything about it!' Of course, if you try to be romantic, right then, she will say something like, 'Too bad, you missed your chance, Buster.' Women are complicated. Especially when they are horny!

Estrogen is the hormone that men curse. It is responsible for the mood swings that women suffer from. If your woman suffers from unpredictable mood swings, if she is loving and nurturing at one moment and the bitch from hell the next, estrogen is your enemy. Not that there is a thing in the world you can do about it, not that you want to anyway. Estrogen is the hormone that makes your woman's vagina all silky and smooth and tight. So stop cursing estrogen! It is what we live for! Anyway, she is only bitchy because you aren't giving her enough!

Let's face it. Sometimes when we are making love to a woman, we might as well be hanging it out of a window there is so little sensation going on. Other times, the sensation is so exquisite, you almost hate to orgasm and be finished. The difference between the two is the amount of estrogen racing around in your honey's blood stream. And it isn't just you. When you can't feel anything, neither can she. When the estrogen is flooding her system in the week before her menses, she is so tight and silky, it makes you feel like a giant to her. You know how women keep a little calendar with important dates on it? Dates like her Mother's birthday or when her next menses is coming? Unless you want to miss some really great sex days, you better start keeping a calendar too; either that or figure out her little code! Look at it this way. Great sex for two week before she bleeds, a week to recover as you both will be so sore, and then a week plus before it starts again, when her vagina gets tighter every day. Those ten days are a great time to practice new techniques and different styles. *(Don't read ahead! If you read this book from start to finish it will be of greater help than if you just read the sexy parts!)*

(For those of you who's woman is beyond the childbearing age, good news! Older women can really get turned on! Plus each time they do, in the back of their mind is the thought that this might be the last time, so they don't want to stop! They will truly go all night with the best of their younger sisters! More in the chapters ahead.)

Two weeks into the ovulation cycle, estrogen production eases off *(don't worry, there is still plenty racing around her blood stream and vagina!)* and progesterone production kicks in. Progesterone is the hormone that makes women horny. In the old days, it made them race around the cave every night collecting sperm from every guy she liked. Make a big circle on your little secret calendar between day 15 and day 28. Your girl is going to be hot to trot and there is still enough estrogen in her body to make her vagina a paradise found. If a girl is ever going to even temporary become a nymphomaniac it is on day 15, 16 and 17. What? Only three days?

What a rip off! I'm not saying she won't want multiple orgasms on other days, I'm saying she really will want to do it all night on those three days. Treasure what you have been given, and also, don't waste it. Don't you dare let the magic days slip by and not do a thing about it! And anyway, are you sure you could handle a nympho every day of the month? You would have to give up watching sports!

Progesterone is the anti-aging hormone. Both men and women produce it, females in vastly greater quantities. *(That's why women live longer!)* In women it increases the mucus in the vagina making it a place where sperm can survive for a long time. *(In case they get lost! Kind of hard to ask directions in the uterus, not that male sperm would want to anyway!) (Ever wonder why there are more females babies? It's because the female sperm ask directions! Forgive me, a little hormone joke there. Ok. A very little joke!)* Besides for making women horny, progesterone makes them beautiful and sexy. Have you ever noticed at work that sometimes your female coworker seems prettier than the week before? More alluring than yesterday? That is progesterone at work. Her hormones are trying to make her the prettiest girl in the cave, for today anyway. *(Both sexes produce all of these hormones. Some a little, some a lot. Much more on this ahead! Some days guys are more handsome than others too!)*

Adrenaline is hormone that gives our bodies that extra energy boost to run away when the saber tooth tiger is attacking or to attack when the same tiger is about to eat your girl. In sex it is a well proven phenomena that when you and your girl are in danger or seem to be in danger, you both feel an increased attraction towards each other. Adrenaline is making us feel this way. People wonder why horror movies are so popular. Next time you go to one, sit in the back where no one can see and play around with your girl while the villain does his thing on the big screen. You will be amazed at how excited you and she will feel. Nothing makes girls feel so horny as the threat of death, even if it is only on the silver screen. After the movie her horniness will last for an extra hour. Pick a movie theater near your house or buy a car with a big back seat! What ever happened to drive ins anyway?

Melanotropin is the hormone that stimulates the tanning process. When your skin is exposed to sunlight, melanotropin is what makes your skin darker. But it does more than that. As thousands of surfers and surf bunnies can tell you, melanotropin suppresses your appetite for fattening food, it triggers an anti-inflammatory reaction in your body so you don't get sick as often, and, most importantly, it triggers sexual desire in both sexes. Many beach bunnies gush over the fact that sun tanning produces 'awesome erections' in their surfer dudes! *(Now you know why people get fat and get the flu during winter!)*

Dopamine is the hormone that keeps you in love. It reacts in the brain much like cocaine, except dopamine is very addictive. Every time you stare into your honey's eyes, you get a shot of dopamine. Unfortunately, the body gets tired of producing this hormone after a varying amount of time and you fall out of love. *(Normally from 3 months to 2 years.)* When you find a new lover, the whole thing starts again. When you fall out of love and your body stops producing dopamine, it is like kicking a cocaine habit cold turkey. Love is a bitch! However every time you make love, the brain produces an extra shot of dopamine especially if you are having multiple orgasms. If you get enough of these shots of dopamine, you and she will never fall out of love. No wonder there are so many nymphomaniacs; they are really drug addicts! *(Much more on the dopamine cycle of 3+ months ahead!)*

Fenylethylamine is a hormone that reacts in the body much like speed does. When you see the one you love or think about him or her, fenylethylamine is produced and makes your heart beat wildly, the palms of your hands get all sweaty, your cheeks and the upper chest of your woman become flooded with blood as, more importantly, do your genitals and nipples. None of these hormones occur by themselves, they cascade in a vast number of concentrations of hormones that can change almost instantly. What this chapter is about, is introducing you to the main sexual hormones so that when I start writing about how to change these hormones you won't be all, 'Huh? What is he talking about now?'

Endorphin is a morphine like hormone that your body produces when you are in pain. It also produces it when you fall in love. Who says that love doesn't hurt? Endorphin reacts in the body much like opium. When you fall out of love and your body stops producing as much endorphin, your girl gets mood swings and feels depressed. *(To stop her from having to quit cold turkey, make love to her, hard and repeatedly. You will be amazed at the good mood swing! Before she was lurking around being a bitch, after she is singing and making you a cocktail!)*

Vasopressin is yet another hormone but is produced in large quantities only in men. However, studies show that vasopressin affects women more. It reacts much like oxytocin does in women. When a man orgasms, vasopressin floods the blood stream and makes the man want to be monogamous. See? Men are the flowers and women the bees! Vasopressin makes a woman want to cuddle after making love. It isn't her, it is her hormones!

Oxytocin, the love hormone, is also the foreplay hormone. When you cuddle or whisper sweet nothings into your girl's ears, she produces oxytocin which takes away fear and makes her feel confident and in control. Many women are unable to orgasm without oxytocin flooding her blood stream first. And here you thought you had to touch each of her special places in the right order. Wrong. You just had to lie next to her and whisper sexy lies *(Oops, I mean sincere truths!)* into her ears.

Serotonin is the hormone that turns off sex or at least the desire for sex. Prozac is an example of a serotonin enhancing drug. Serotonin is released by the brain when we become depressed and when it is released we become less depressed. A woman who is happily making love and then suddenly doesn't want to continue, just received a shot of serotonin. She didn't do it voluntarily. Her brain did it all by itself. *(However, serotonin laced with vasopressin also makes her want to cuddle. Cuddling increases her oxytocin which makes her want to do it again. Women are complicated! So when she wants to cuddle, just do it, Dude. And whisper in her ear!)*

A major mystery of women is why they are so difficult to excite to orgasm especially compared to men. When we study serotonin it becomes more obvious. Back in the day, back in the cave, the woman in week 3 of her cycle is making the rounds of all the men in the cave, one after the other. Some have no trouble making her orgasm, others don't seem to be able. This is a survival adaptation for a cave woman. The man who goes to the trouble to find and play with all her 'turn on' spots, or who will at least cuddle her first and whisper lies, will have little trouble bringing her to orgasm. The guy who just rams it in, does his thing and then just tosses her away will cause the woman's brain to release serotonin every time she sees him. If it is a really tough cave, she might be wandering around in a serotonin laced dream. The chances of her becoming pregnant are slim not only because she is getting laid less, but also because serotonin makes the body stop producing estrogen and progesterone. She can't get pregnant. This is to protect the woman. If there is no man to protect her and provide for her, how is she going to care for a child? It is better if she didn't get pregnant at all. In fact, logic demands that she wander off and find a new cave. This is exactly what is found in the blood steams of teenage runaways. They are loaded with serotonin. And here are the frantic parents worried that she is shacking up with a boy friend. Wrong! The last thing she wants right now is a romantic boy friend.

Dehydroepiandrosterone, DHEA for short *(thank god!)*, is the hormone that is released when making love that makes us orgasm by spiking 3 to 5 times it's normal level. Making love, using all those other hormones, is a lot of fun but it is DHEA that rings our bell and your honey's, too. Have you ever made love and just couldn't get off? Lack of DHEA, Dude! You need to pay attention when I talk about this one!

Pheromones aren't hormones. They are an odorless, tasteless chemical produced by the body to signal to the opposite sex that you are ready and willing to procreate. Body odor is not an example of a pheromone. In fact, body odor masks pheromones as will heavily scented soaps. Both sexes seem to like to wear perfumes or musk. Both are a failure. All they do is mask your pheromones that are telling the world that you want to get laid. If you do feel you have to wear perfume, make it a very light one. Some perfumes brag that they are an artificial form of pheromone. However unlikely that may be, the purpose of pheromones is to tell the people around you, who you are and what you are looking for. They are like a sign on your forehead stating that you want to get laid and you have a cave the two of you can use.

Pheromones are produced by all of the skin but are concentrated in the armpit and genital areas. They are perceived by the opposite sex in the upper reaches of the nasal cavities. These scents stir up ancient behaviors reaching back hundreds of thousands of years. *(If you believe in Darwinism. Like me!)* The brain is not involved. If you ever find yourself walking down a strange street for no good reason at all and are starting to become aroused, there is a very good chance that a pheromone is in the air and your body is taking control and hunting down the source!

Alright. Let's put all of this information in a format we can understand. How do all these hormones help us get laid? How will these hormones find us a girl that will screw our brains out all night long? How can we induce the hormones we want into the pristine and perfect body of our little sweethearts? How can we turn our girls into sex machines? Read on, Stud! Your fabulous future is ahead of you! You is one lucky Dude!

Mystery Woman
A True Story

I never knew her name. I met her on a bus in Hawaii going from one side of the island to the other. She was visiting from the 'Mainland' as Hawaiians call the other 49 States of the USA. She was pretty, cute and about my own age, 24. We got to talking. I want to make one thing perfectly clear, *(to quote some old politician)* I am not some kind of Adonis or Satyr. I am your average Joe, maybe with a streak of stubbornness. Mostly I make love once a day, if that. As the bus approached Kaneohe Bay, where my small boat was anchored, I asked her, without much hope, if she cared to see my boat. She accepted in a gentle, quiet, polite way. Who would have guessed?

Once on the boat I discovered that she had all the pieces in the right places. She wasn't like Hollywood gorgeous or super built or anything. Neither did she have a mustache. I don't remember which ways we made love first. I do remember that we couldn't stop. We made love 23 times in 10 hours. I remember that because my Mystery Woman was keeping score on a piece of paper. She brought out the beast in me!

She didn't want to stop after 23, but she did want a shower and to grab some lubricant. *(I was sailing on a 24 foot Columbia Challenger in those days, a bucket was the head and the shower was the ocean.)* I rowed her ashore as she wanted us to go to her house and then I chickened out. I was so sore! I was tired. And I wanted to go to sleep! I know, I should have gone. But what a great memory just the way it was!

One thing I did learn, Nymphomaniacs do exist! Desire, wanting someone special in your life, or more accurately, your girl wanting you to be her someone special is driven by the following hormones in the next chapter.

Hormones and Sex

Sex comes in five waves. Five tidal waves. Five tsunamis! They are:

Desire, the wanting of an encounter;
Lust, having found someone, wanting her, sexually;
Love, realizing special feelings for a certain someone;
Sex, having orgasmic relations with someone;
Attachment, ignoring other potential mates, saving yourself
    sexually for your special one.

Each of these tsunamis are driven by different hormones and combinations of hormones. Just because you meet a girl in a bar and she smiles at you, doesn't necessary mean that she is ready to get down and dirty with you. She may well do so, but other hormones will have to come into play before she will. You can influence the cascade of hormones in her blood stream at any time. With experience you can encourage the hormone mix to repeat tsunamis number 4 as many times as you wish. You can turn your girl into a raving nymphomaniac!

First, a warning. You are not standing outside the box in a white lab coat writing notes on a clipboard. You are in the box with the girl and she can influence you as much as you can her. She can push your buttons, she can change your hormone cascade as much as you can hers. Proceed with caution!

Second, an explanation. Influencing her hormone cascade isn't going to happen over and over again unless she has the building blocks, the nutritional supplies to create new hormones. We will delve into this subject later instead of now in the interest of clarity even though they are fingers on the same hand. In other words, don't read part of this book, go out and try out what you learned, and then blame me because it didn't work or didn't work repeatedly. This is a complicated subject. Either memorize important parts or create your own Cliff notes for use if you find yourself somehow distracted when a clear mind is needed.

Third, a realization. You are dealing with real people here. What you do to a woman is going to stay with her for the rest of her life. If you go messing with her and destroy her happiness, turn her into a vixen, it is your duty to fix what you have created. Don't leave a trail of broken hearts in your wake. Not only is it cruel but you have no idea what they are going to do to you in Hell for all of eternity! *(If you believe in Creationism.)*

Alright then. Let's get into it. Imagine, if you will, a bar. There is a girl sitting on a stool, alone. Your mission, if you choose to accept it, is to meet her and to get her phone number. That is all this mission is about. One step at a time and don't skip steps!

_/) _/) _/)

Desire, wanting of romantic love is a strange time in a girl's hormone stream. She has low testosterone but high oxytocin levels. Testosterone makes her more aggressive in getting what she wants, oxytocin makes her more receptive to any advance by another. So, yes, she sits there in the bar waiting for you to make the first move. It isn't that she is shy, her lack of testosterone is making her act that way. Her serotonin levels are half way up the scale. This protects her from rejection. Serotonin makes her feel like she doesn't really want to meet someone anyway. Serotonin is your enemy in this part of your relationship. She will feel a spike of adrenaline as you approach her. Remember, she can't help it. These hormones are hardwired into her motherboard. There really isn't anyway she can influence the way they work at least if she hasn't read this book. If the girl you approach is playing hard to get, if her serotonin levels are high, she still will get that same jolt of adrenaline however serotonin is just able to mask it better.

Depending where she is in her ovulation cycle, she is loaded with either estrogen or progesterone. The difference in the two is slight but important. In later tsunamis, these two hormones are going to be far more important. For now with her system loaded with oxytocin, if she has recently ovulated, estrogen is making her more permissive allowing her to let others touch her hands, shoulders or to ask her questions. If she is going to soon ovulate, progesterone is making her more receptive, her hormones are allowing her to get to know you better, under the influence of progesterone she will ask you questions about yourself rather than just sit there fielding pop flies and not throwing any back. These are important points if you are looking for a nymphomaniac. Remember, if she asks questions, she is laden with progesterone; if she wants you to do all the work, she is bursting with estrogen. Both are good but you need to know where she is in her cycle if you are going to change her hormone cascade.

An important fact to remember about the estrogen-progesterone mix; if you don't like what you see, wait two weeks and a slightly different girl will be sitting on the stool! If you date a girl and she is a meek and quiet door mouse and then two weeks later she is staring between your legs, she isn't necessarily suddenly in lust with you. In another two weeks the door mouse will be back.

Her melanotropin is low. Remember it is created by sunlight. Anytime a girl asks you to walk on the beach with her, jump at it! She is happy on the beach because melanotropin makes her feel sexy. Yes, she is just as sexy if not more so sitting on her stool at the bar wearing a skimpy little cocktail dress but stop thinking with your lower head. What matters is how sexy *she* feels. The sexier she feels, the more likely that she will give you her phone number.

All the other hormones are low except for pheromones. Pheromones aren't hormones, they are chemicals released by the body that cause powerful hormonal cascades in the opposite sex. Pheromones can change our behavior in a heartbeat. Humans, actually almost all mammals, release and sense pheromones 24/7, even in your sleep. In unusual situations, like sitting on a bar stool, a girl is particularly sensitive to these chemicals. You can't smell them. They aren't sweat, they aren't body odor. But they sure can influence us. *(By the way, heavy perfume and strong scented soap like Irish Spring can mask pheromones. Don't use them when picking up girls at a bar!)* Pheromones are individual. They are like a sign on our foreheads telling the world who and what we are, at that moment. If you are secretively nervous in the bar walking over to the girl on the stool, don't hide it. She is going to know you are nervous anyway from your pheromones and when you hide it all she will sense is that you are evading, that you are hiding something. Make sure you are in a good mood, are happy and are out for a good time talking to a nice girl at a bar. She will sense this in your pheromones and the battle is mostly won all without speaking a word!

Men always ask, 'What do I say to a girl?' What you say counts, at the most ten percent of the girl's decision of whether or not to give you her phone number. An effective way to pick up chicks is to stare into their eyes, non stop, for 3 or 4 minutes. She might look away, but trust me, she will look back. Look intently into her eyes, nowhere else. Don't stare mindlessly. Try to read who she is from the depths of her eyes. After 4 minutes either stand up and take her hand or simply say, 'Shall we?' Either way lead her to somewhere quiet, the more natural the better. When dealing with hormones and pheromones, the brain really isn't involved! Actually the brain is in charge of making the hormones or directing that they be made, but this is a different part of the brain than the thinking part. It is a primal part of the brain that developed back when we were lizards or what ever. *(Being a Darwinian sure is more fun! Personally I am sure I am descended from a Mastodon!)* During those 3 or 4 minutes she is 'reading' your pheromones. She isn't doing it intentionally. If your particular pheromones are what her hormones are looking for, you have a date without ever speaking a word!

If when talking to the girl on the stool, you somehow manage to make her laugh delightedly *(not sarcastically)* she will get a spike of dopamine. When she does, make sure you are staring into each other's eyes or your are touching her hand or have some kind of contact. Dopamine as I am sure you still remember *(you are reading this book from front to back aren't you?)* gives her a little jolt of a hormone very like cocaine. If you can keep making contact during the dopamine shot, in a very short time she will become addicted to you. Well, actually she will become addicted to your touch or to you gazing into her eyes. And like any drug addict, she will go to great lengths to get her next fix.

Right now, sitting on her stool, her dopamine levels are very low, most likely because she is bored and is getting zero action. Good thing you walked over, isn't it? Poor thing is in withdrawal!

_/) _/) _/)

Alright, Mission Impossible Trainee, you obtained her phone number and it is the next day. The object of this next mission, if you choose to accept it, is to phone her up and set up a time and place for a date. You must use the word, 'Date'. Guys don't make a big distinction between hanging out with a girl and taking her on a date. Girls do. They will dress differently, prepare differently and most important of all, meet you with a wildly different hormone cascade for a date than she would if she is just hanging out. Tell her that you are taking her to the carnival. The one with all those scary rides. If you have been paying attention, you know why.

_/) _/) _/)

Lust: having found someone and wanting them sexually. If your bar girl agrees to come out on a date with you she is at least toying with the idea of making love with you. Almost for sure she hasn't made up her mind yet. However her hormone cascade is going to be wildly different than the first time you met. It is important not to think she is going to behave like the same girl she was in the bar. Well, of course, she is the same girl, however her different hormones are going to make her act differently.

On a date, even with a new man, her hormones are switching around, depending on how the date is going, between the possibility of entering into a romantic relationship or simply experiencing some heavy petting, maybe even if the date is going really well, she is thinking about showing you a really good time, going all the way. Or all of the above. In any case the most profound difference in her hormone cascade is the presence of testosterone. Testosterone in women make them more aggressive in stating their desires and even making the first move. Testosterone also activates her clitoris making her aware of it. She might think that you are such a stud, you are making her feel this way. The truth is she started the testosterone cascade when she left her house to meet you. No, actually, her cascade started when she dressed for the date. Girls make such a big deal about what clothes to wear because what she wears can change what hormones are in her blood, changing how she feels. *(If she asks you what she should wear, always say something sexy and comfortable. The two are fairly incompatible. This is good. She will spend hours deciding if she wants to be comfortable or sexy with you. Either one at this stage is a win for us!)* Her oxytocin levels are still high making her laugh easily at your jokes and happily hold your hand. Maybe stand with the side of her body touching yours. Her serotonin has fallen to all time lows making her more than willing to try new experiences. Every time you surprise her she will get a little jolt of adrenaline. Especially if you take her to the carnival and take her on the roller coaster. Mentally, she knows that the adrenaline she is experiencing is caused by the ride. Her hormones think it is because of her proximity to you. Every time you go on a ride and she gets a adrenaline spike and since she doesn't die, her hormones think it is because you are protecting her. Remember, you are not wooing her at this time, you are wooing her hormones!

Right now her estrogen and progesterone levels are being controlled with all the oxytocin she is cascading. Oxytocin is waking up her sexual desires. Estrogen and/or progesterone are telling her to be more receptive and permissive towards you. Oxytocin is telling her that it is going ahead and getting her ready for love. Oxytocin is being cascaded by the high levels of adrenaline caused by the feelings of near death *(her hormones think)* the rides are giving her. Her vagina is getting moist, her eyes are dilating, her nipples are hardening and her nostrils are flaring. Remember, she is not thinking of making love to you, her hormones are getting her ready as they think you are saving her from saber tooth tigers and when you buy her popcorn or cotton candy, you are feeding her. Mentally she probably thinks you are a cheapo for not taking her to dinner and a movie. Hormonally, she feels that you are a hero! Mentally you are being added to her list of possible future dates, but it doesn't matter. She doesn't know it but her hormones are in charge of her behavior. And you have the key!

Every time your car on the roller coaster screeches around a corner or dives down a big hill, grab her around the waist and stare into her eyes. Scream together if you like. Each time the car screeches, she will get a little jolt of dopamine. Dopamine is the hormone that makes her fall in love with you. If you are not interested in her socially, just sexually, every time you go around a corner, hold her breast 'accidentally' or place your palm over her nipple, not hard, not groping. Just make contact, accidentally, like. Remember to take your hand away when the car returns to the straight and narrow. Dopamine is addictive. In the first case she is becoming addicted to you staring into her eyes, in the second case addicted to you touching her sexually. A little of each is the best of both worlds.

Both of you are producing plenty of pheromones on the rides. Make sure you don't take her on rides that scare you. You want her to sense you as a protector and savior. If you can, go the carnival earlier in the week, get used to the rides and practice throwing darts or tossing rings around a bottle. It would really help if you could win her a teddy bear. You would be a real provider then!

The hormones of lust are more than sex organ hormones. Wait. That isn't right. Phenylethylamine *(PEA for short. Think, Phenyl ethyl amine)* is a hormone of the brain. PEA isn't a sex hormone, it is the hormone of illusion! The brain is the biggest sex organ in the human body. A girl can have all the hormones in the world racing around in her blood stream and she still will sit there in front of the TV pouting. Television is the great killer of romance and sex. Turn on the box any time of day. Ads will be showing people just like you with bags under your eyes, saggy breasts, pain almost everywhere, serious problems in your insides, fallen arches, dandruff, sciatica, split ends, erectile dysfunction, piles, hemorrhoids and the list goes on and on and on. Then the program comes on with Miss America class starlets in various states of undress showing their perfect bodies. Is there any wonder that women look at their own bodies and say, 'I am as ugly as they come.' And 'Everything is wrong with me.' Or 'No one could ever love me.'

Fear not! PEA to the rescue! Phenylethylamine is the hormone that tells the brain that it lives inside the most beautiful body in the universe! And the miracle is, the brain believes it! Let's not listen to those that say hormones have no power! The PEA laced brain looks in the mirror and ignores all the imperfections, it notices instead the left ear. What a beautiful ear! What a beautiful girl! Every guy is going to be dying to dance with me tonight! Me and my ear are beautiful!

The thing is, they will. Her pheromones are going to be broadcasting that I am beautiful and if you play your cards right, you might get lucky! Nothing is as sexy as self confidence!

Women are often dysfunctional when it comes to awareness of desire. When standing next to a stranger at the train station, their bodies can be sexually active, their clitorises engorged, their nipples excited and sensitized, their vaginas moist and their brain thinking only of what to feed the kids for dinner. This is difficult for a man to believe but study after study has confirmed its validity. When a man is aroused he most definitely is aware of it. No question about it. A woman's brain needs to be romanced before she is aware of what her body is feeling. Equally well, a woman may be shouting at her mate without realizing that she is even raising her voice. Her brain is disassociated from her body when emotions are running wild in her hormone cascade. Scientists have scratched their heads for centuries trying to discover why this is so. It was not until the study of hormones and pheromones and their play in human sexuality had their turn at bat that a light started to shine dimly at the end of the tunnel. People used to think that sexual desire was driven by the brain. Today, simple experiments show that the human body of both sexes can react to pheromones without the brain having the slightest idea of what is happening. Why there is little or no communication from the body to the brain in stressful moments is a mystery. Certainly there is communication from the brain to the body. Any man can tell you that if the radio playing music next to the bed where he and his girl are happily making love, starts giving sports score, his erection starts to fade. His attention is partially divided. Why can't the body tell the brain, 'Hey, I'm busy here! Bug out!' But it can't, so it doesn't.

Equally well, when a woman is screaming in an argument, she is unaware that she is even raising her voice and will vehemently deny it if accused. Again this is a sexual problem. Women rarely argue unless sexually frustrated. *(An interesting experiment that you can perform in your own bedroom will highlight the above statement, if you have doubts of it validity. The next time your girl raises her voice and starts to argue, throw her on the bed, or table or whatever, and make love to her. You will be startled at the outcome. She will fight you, tooth and nail while you are doing her, but after you come and especially if you make her orgasm, what a sea change! She will be docile, she will be singing, she will make your favorite foods. It is the only real way to win an argument with a woman!)* Her brain may well be supplying the words of the argument but her body is supplying the emotional content. And her brain is unaware of the emotions her body is projecting.

What is happening is cortisol is ruling her cascade with an unhealthy dose of testosterone. The testosterone is telling her that she wants sex in the worse way but the cortisol is directing her that she is not going to get it ever again. No wonder the poor creature is confused. We would be too! Making love to her appeases her testosterone. At least now she doesn't have two hormones shouting in her inner ear. When a guy comes he injects not only sperm but also a mix of hormones into the vagina including oxytocin and estrogen, both enemies of cortisol. The simple act of making love solves the problem. Maybe those hippies had the right idea, make love not war, except it should have read, make love to stop war!

_/) _/) _/)

Love: She is falling in love with you. This is not hard. Girls are predisposed to fall in love. In fact when they are not in love, they are very unhappy creatures. When she does fall in love two hormones are going dominate her hormone cascade.

Oxytocin is the love hormone. It is the main player when a girl, or a guy, is in love. Especially when she is in that special time for love, the first three months with a new lover. Dopamine is the hormone that says, in those first three months: make love as often as you can. Dopamine is the nymphomaniac hormone!

Those first three months of love are what the poets write about. Love doesn't get much better than those few months. But first a correction of a common sexual misunderstanding based on the fact that men and women speak different languages. Men when they want to make love, grab the girl and say, 'Let's have some fun,' do the sexual deed and then will put up with a few seconds of cuddling before going to sleep. Women on the other hand will first want to have fun, then want to cuddle, then want to get down and lusty and then, after, want to have a long lasting cuddle leading to further bouts of love interspaced with more cuddling. For the first 3 months the guy will go along with the girl's ideas. Then the novelty wears off. He isn't a stranger anymore. Her levels of adrenaline aren't as high as she is fairly sure he isn't a serial killer by now, she doesn't have to be ready to run away. Dopamine levels are also falling. The body can't produce dopamine forever, or more properly, all hormones need receptor spots where they can plug into to do their job. Dopamine, when it finds a spot, likes to hang out and shoot the breeze with the other hormones passing by. Its work is done, it should be running for second so the hitter has a base to run to but he is a good old boy and likes to hang out. After a while, all the receptor spots are filled up and until the body can evict an old dopamine molecule, new ones can't get in and do their job. Your girl starts to take you for granted.

Survival in the old caveman days depended on dopamine. It made sure that however much you loved Ughy over there in the corner, if you didn't get her pregnant within 3 months or so, she would fall out of love and find someone new. Stands to reason, a cave had to have children to support the batch of current hunters and gatherers as they aged or were killed by an astonishing number of predators. Women are genetically predisposed to fall out of love if she doesn't become pregnant and/or she is getting less action in the sack. Of course it isn't that easy.

All other mammals have periods of 'heat' where the female's body is ready for love and dopamine soars in males and females. *(Yes, Virginia, all mammals have hormones, just like you and me. What? You thought God made you special? Actually, man is special. He likes to kill, loves to, often needlessly. Dolphins have bigger brains, octopus can think just as well if not better, most everything can climb and run better. If God is all merciful, why did he make a child in his image, a natural born killer?)* Other mammals are sexually indifferent except in times of 'heat', otherwise it would be this massive love fest morning to evening and who needs sleep anyway. Animals with their brains electronically hardwired to give them a jolt of dopamine ignore food, ignore water, ignore everything; they just keep pushing that little lever that gives them their fix. Human females don't have that preventive 'heat' pause wired into them. Instead, she falls out of love, cries a little, eats a lot, *(Presumably she has been f_king her brains out and has forgotten to eat)* and then after a while find a new 'someone special' and start all over again until she gets pregnant! The human genetic code wins again! The species will survive!

OK. You are on your date. Unless you are mean or cruel to her, she will fall in love with you, at least a little bit. It isn't like she has a choice, that is what women do, they fall in love. It doesn't matter what you say or do. Women love to fall in love. She wouldn't have been sitting on that bar stool, alone, if she wasn't ready for someone new.

It really helps if you are her provider. That is what her hormones are looking for, a provider. Someone to feed her, someone to put a roof over her head, someone to build her a nest. Your girl does have a life apart from her hormones. She will want a guy that can make her laugh. It was a cold hard life spending a winter in a cave with a guy with no sense of humor! She wants a guy who is in love with her, who loves to stare into her eyes. That gives her confidence that when you go out hunting, you will bring her the catch, not that girl in the next cave over. She wants to be sure that you will last the winter thru. However, if she doesn't get pregnant, when spring comes she will be ready to fall in love with someone new.

Women have been characterized as being devious in their dealings with others. I'm not sure about the use of the verb, but absolutely. They are always out looking for a new sugar daddy, a new provider as soon as you are not measuring up. They have been playing this game of the power behind the throne since girlhood and often don't want to give it up. They flirt, sure, it is in their nature; you might as well ask a bird not to fly. Just because they are flirting doesn't necessarily mean they are looking for the next Mr. Right, but it also doesn't mean that they aren't. They aren't behaving from directives from their brain. Their hormones are making them flirt. When you see your girl flirting, ask yourself, 'Have I been the best provider I can be?' Are you sure you have? Providing for a girl isn't what you might think.

She expects you to clothe her. Be careful. Giving her money to go shopping is not the same as going to the store with her. Once the money is in her little hot hands, she is in command. She is now clothing herself. You aren't. Go with her. Retain the veto on her selections. You are doing the supplying. When she shows you her selection, posing for you, run your hands over it on her. Don't just look. Let her hormones be very sure who is doing the buying. I know, that you know, that she knows who her Daddy is, but never forget that her brain turns off during sex and her hormones take over. How wild she is and how many times she wants to do it, and how many different ways she does it, is being determined by her hormones, not the brain that watched you buy her clothes.

She expects you to feed her. If you give her money to go to the grocery store, the same as above, once the money is in her purse, she is feeding herself. Go to the store with her. Be sure to pick out man foods: beer, chips, hot dogs, chili. If she complains, start taking out her vegetables from the cart. You are in charge. Make her use her feminine wiles to get you to buy her stuff. Make her flirt with you to get her way. Girls will flirt, it is their way, make sure you are the target of her flirting. At the cash register, take the bills but give her the coins. Her hormones will feel that you are giving her independence. An independent girl is a lot more fun in the sack! It doesn't matter that the 15 cents you give her isn't going to last long, her hormones will be in love with you! The brain and the hormones live in different worlds. No wonder women are complicated!

She expects you to house her. Be prepared, no matter how nice your house or apartment is, she will want to change it. She is making her nest. All girls do this. Don't fight it. You won't win. It is a feminine trait. She will want her own space. This usually includes the bedroom and the kitchen. Don't fight this either. You might win but you will lose the girl. If she wants you to wash the dishes in her kitchen, make sure she realizes that you are only doing it to get a free feel now and then. Never forget to touch and feel, stroke and pet. Always remind her hormones that she is a sexual creature. Her hormones will agree. They like to turn her into a nymphomaniac, it is their role in life. Their code is: screw your brains out until you get pregnant! It may well be that she doesn't want children. No ifs, ands or buts. It is her brain that doesn't want children. Her hormones most definitely do. Such is the mixed up body that she lives in! When you are screwing her brains out and she suddenly blurts out, "Give me a baby, Honey, put a baby in me!" she hasn't changed her mind. Woman's brains turn off during sex. That was her hormones talking. She will remember what she said later and wonder why she ever said such a thing.

If you take what she says during sex seriously, she will start to pull away from sex. She will distrust her body. She will fear what her body might do when she is making love. For example, in the throes of passion, she might say, "Screw me in the ass!" Later, when her brain is in control, and the subject comes up, she will say, "I hated it in the ass. Keep that thing away from me!" People say that women are complicated, but they really aren't, they are perfectly rational when their brains are in control.

Rereading the above, I realize that I said 'get her pregnant' too often. It isn't important that you get her pregnant as it is that you screw her every chance you get. If you act like you are trying to get her pregnant, her hormones will love you!

Okay, she really liked her date with you. More than that, you might even have qualified for Mr. Right as I'm sure that you provided for her properly, winning her a stuffed teddy bear at the amusement park. Her hormones are in a fever to not only kiss you, but to go all the way. Forget about getting to first, second or third base. You just hit a home run!

_/) _/) _/)

Sex is what women live for. I know, men live for sex too, but not like women. Men rave on and on about getting their rocks off and how great it feels. They have no idea about how intense a woman's orgasm is. If fact, authorities don't even call a man's ejaculation an orgasm. It is like calling a high school football team equal to a professional team. Not in the same league. So when you give an orgasm to your girl, it is really a big thing. The very best thing about a girl's orgasm is it chases serotonin away. The hormone serotonin is your enemy. This hormone turns her fun loving sex hormones off and makes your girl very depressed. If your honey is high on serotonin when you give her a feel in the kitchen, you might get a frying pan across the face. When you asked her how she wanted her steak cooked, it was serotonin that made her burst into tears and want her mother.

Much of the study of getting into a girl's pants, to say it in the vernacular, is learning how to fight serotonin. It isn't an easy fight, but since you will be fighting it your entire married life, and even before, we might as well get into it.

Serotonin inhibits orgasm and clitoral and penile erection. Your love life is going to be close to non-existent if your honey is depressed by high levels of serotonin. More than that, as she will be bitchy, crabby, nasty, argumentive, back biting and cruel, she will be next to impossible to live with. Once serotonin raises its ugly head, you and your girl are going to descend into the living hell of an sexually dysfunctional relationship. Before you get on a rant, it is equally possible for a man to suffer from a serotonin depression. It may be you that is the problem, not her; however it is far more common for a female to suffer this terrible infliction.

Often doctors prescribe Prozac and its kin for depression which *increases* the levels of serotonin in the blood stream! They do this because serotonin lowers the bodies levels of dopamine and adrenaline, the brain exciters, which blunts the emotions. Without emotions a person just isn't going to get laid. She is not sending out the right signals. Hell, a serotonin laden girl would never have been sitting on that bar stool in the first place.

So why do our bodies even make serotonin in the first place? A serotonin laden depression is a clear call for help. 'Something is wrong with me and with this relationship. Please do something!' Often when a relationship is failing, for one reason or another, serotonin kicks in and makes it so miserable that the couple have no choice but to split. What happens when a guy really truly loves a girl but he can't give her any children that she really wants? *(If she doesn't want children, it is a different story. These biological adaptive behaviors were developed in the dawn of humankind when the survival of the species depended on as many off spring as possible were conceived, successfully born and lovingly reared.)* She gets depressed. She is forced to become depressed. Her body floods her system with serotonin, there is no way she can't be depressed. Her body is forcing her to end her relationship with her guy and to find a new man that might give her a child. She might not want a child, but I kid you not, her hormones most definitely do!

Slightly heightened serotonin levels are a good thing. Almost all newlyweds have heightened serotonin levels. This takes them off the dating circuit, it makes them blind to their mate's faults, whatever they may be, and makes them believe that their love is unique and more powerful then all of the loves the world has every known.

Love is complicated. Very. Here the same hormone that can destroy a relationship can in the early stages protect it. This in spite of, no doubt, prolific orgasms of both partners.

Making love is the destroyer of serotonin. A man's seminal fluid, released with the sperm in orgasm, contains quite significant amounts of dopamine, adrenaline, vasopressin, testosterone and estrogen. These are all sex hormones. Each time a girl makes love, her guy injects these hormones into her vagina. No wonder she wants to wander about the cave and find another lover. Her significant other just unintentionally encouraged her to do so. If you can stay awake and make love to your honey at least three times once a week, she will never suffer from serotonin depression. If there is one paragraph you should retain from this book, it is the one above. This paragraph will solve 99% of relationship problems. All women are nymphomaniacs, or at least they are once a week! Try it. You will suddenly be surprised that your bride you once considered divorcing is suddenly the girl you fell in love with so many years ago! Who knew it was so easy!

_/) _/) _/)

Attachment, loving each other during the long years of raising the kids is the last of the hormonal cascades and one of the most important ones. The fire of passion of the early few years has faded and in its place is, hopefully, a shared feeling of mutual love. It isn't automatic. When you first fell in love, your bodies were designed to go all out; to love and to make love. After 3 months there is a drop in the automatic part, and after 2 years the automatic bit has managed to disappear. What is called the first blush of love has fallen off the rose and is lying there wilting on the ground. That doesn't mean you don't love each other just as much, just that it isn't automatic. Now you have to work at it. Damn!

Now you have to plan ahead. Well, with kids running around your ankles you definitely have to plan ahead. Even if you don't have kids yet, you still have to think before acting. It isn't easy. He doesn't look at her naked and get an instantaneous hard on. She doesn't melt when he wraps her in his arms, blood rushing, eyes unfocusing. They still love each other. It just isn't automatic.

If you run your hands down her back, fingers through her hair, you will feel the old feelings coming back. Rubbing her skin increases your testosterone levels. It doesn't work that way for her. She can rub your back for all she is worth, and as nice as it feels, nothing will happen. Her oxytocin levels will be rock steady, they might even decrease a tad. However if she thinks about being loving towards you, if she acts on her thoughts, if she makes a meal she knows you will enjoy, picks out a video she hopes pleases you, her oxytocin levels will soar.   Often, if she hasn't orgasmed recently, her serotonin levels have creeped up, she is stressed out. Maybe even depressed a bit with her life. She will feel that everything depends on her when in reality a part of her wants to be the free and happy little girl she once was or at least the star struck woman of just a few years ago. The only thing that can bring her back to an even keel is making love, but all the stress in her life is preventing her from feeling the slightest bit interested. Bummer, huh?

This will be her life for all her childbearing years, and maybe even beyond. It is up to you to help her out. No, no, no. Don't wash the dishes, cook for the kids or vacuum the house. In her depressed state, while she may thank you, you will not help her stressed out self one bit. She will just think that she will have to do it all over again because there is no way that you would have of done it correctly. *(Stress is an evil mental state.)* Instead, plan ahead, one day a week, and take her out on a date, just the two of you. Yes, you will have to pay for a baby sitter; yes, you will have to take her to a fancy dinner and a first rate movie; but look at the bright side. She will soon become the wild sexy creature she once was, her stress will evaporate almost instantly, your life will be good again and there will be laughter and giggling in your bed once, or multiple times more.

Stress is the marriage/relationship killer. Every time she is stressed out, actually, if you can, before she is stressed out, give her a good night out and leave no doubt in her mind that you think she is the most attractive, beautiful, sexist woman in the world. Make her believe it. Don't even glance at another woman all night long. Practice not looking before hand. Play hanky panky under the table cloth like you did when you were teenagers. Then take her home, long after the kids are asleep and make wild passionate love to her as many times as you can. She will cry, 'Enough already!' Don't believe her. Don't you dare stop. *(If you need hints, check out a great book, this books companion, "How to Turn Your 60+ Man into a Red Hot Lover.....For Females Only." Written, actually, by the same author! It's for females only because, frankly, a guy will have a hard time reading all the details of the techniques of making love. Wait. There are some pictures. Maybe it is for men too!)* Anyway, a night like this will put her back on an even keel for weeks if not a month.

In a serotonin depression, she will believe that the fun dating years are gone for her. Don't let it happen. Give her candy and flowers, sure. But be insistent that she pay the price. If you give her a gift and then ignore her and turn on the boob tube, you would be better off if you never gave her anything at all. The gift for her is just the first step in the dance of seduction, a dance that was her favorite in her late teens and early twenties. She is sitting there at home, her hair hanging down and in her grubby jeans, pouting. Yes, I know that is a turn on for you. It isn't for her. She wants to dress up. She wants to have a reason to dress up. She wants to be seduced. She wants to be chased. She wants to be caught and ravished. Instead, she is changing diapers and doing the same chores at home she has done hundreds of times before while all the starlets of TV are having all the fun.

Planning a date, thinking about it, increases your testosterone levels. You are going to be ready, yes, sir! Unfortunately, when you tell her that the two of you are going out on a date she will be even more stressed out. She will just see all the problems involved. Whatever you do, don't ask her where she wants to go. Trying to decided will increase her stress levels. Stress, of course, leads to depression. Decide for her. Tell her how you want her to dress. Casual for a movie, a bit fancier for a nice restaurant, a lose flowing dress for a drive in if you can find one in this world gone mad! When her depression has eased a bit, tell her you don't want her to wear any panties. Her clothes will rub against her clitoris making her aware of what all her hormones are shouting. She is the seducee, you are the pursuer. She wants to be chased, she wants to be caught. Boy, the two of you are going to have a lot of fun!

Oxytocin, the love hormone, is the natural enemy of cortisol, the stress hormone. You thought life was tough enough with just serotonin to deal with. Guess what, the deck is stacked against you. *BUT!* But you are allowed to stack the deck. You will have to cheat to beat cortisol. Both of you have oxytocin racing through your blood stream, she has more than you. She needs more, women are prone to worrying. Women, far more than men, are subject to the evil effects of cortisol. If you have a two year old child and she starts talking about what college she should go to, she isn't being silly, she is talking through a cortisol haze. Don't fall into her depression. Don't talk rationally about it. Take her in your arms and kiss her neck. *(Remember, at this stage of her life, body contact isn't going to do it for her, but she will feel your excitement and sense your pheromones change.)* Ask her to make you what ever food comes into your mind. It doesn't matter what. Asking her to do something personal for you will increase her oxytocin levels which will lower her cortisol level and all will be right with your world and, hopefully, hers. If she rears up on her back legs and refuses, she is in a deep depression indeed. At that point there is only one solution, a risky one. If any women are reading this they are going to cry, rape. More or less that is exactly what you have to do. Toss her on the bed and do a life saving deed. This is one of the reasons that husbands cannot be tried for rape against their wives, some times there is just no other solution. But it is risky. You might alienate her and risk divorce. In today's lily livered world, many men send their wives to a psychiatrist who will talk to them forever at $300 an hour and then prescribe serotonin enhancing drugs! It is true. The reason is if you increase a woman's depression, she will be so depressed she won't have the energy to do any harm to herself or her children. It is a lot more effective to make love to her repeatedly. And way more fun!

In a way turning your wife into a nymphomaniac might be the healthiest thing you can do for her. Not a nympho every night of the week, but at least one night a month, preferably on the cusp of her cycle. You may be more than willing to do this but the body can't come up to bat. Bear in mind that you don't have to be a satyr *(a male nymphomaniac)*, she has to come multiple times, given time you might come twice. If you feel ripped off, we will talk about how you can trick your body into having more erections more often in a couple of chapters.

And here you thought turning your wife into a raving nymphomaniac was all for your pleasure; turns out it can be the healthiest thing you can do for your girl.

The Evil Demon Cortisol

Cortisol is the cause of most of the evil in the world. Certainly it is the cause of most of the unhappiness in women. Just about every thing that goes wrong in a woman's body is started by a sudden increase of the hormone, cortisol. Cortisol does the following:

Suppresses her immune system
Increase the occurrence of yeast infections
Turns off her cancer fighting T and NK cells
Tremendously increases the chances of breast cancer
Increases blood pressure and heart disease
Rewires the neurons in your brain and
Makes it difficult to remember things
Causes adult onset diabetes
Causes Alzheimer's disease
Causes ulcers
Causes irritable Bowel syndrome
Causes arthritis
Causes a loss of skin elasticity
Causes osteoporosis
Reduces her metabolic rate
Dries out her skin

Ready for the bad news? Men suffer from cortisol also. Maybe not as much as women, but we will get all of the above. *(well, maybe not the yeast infections and breast cancer!)*

Cortisol is the stress hormone and causes intense depressions in women. So which comes first, cortisol or serotonin? Serotonin certainly, which is why we have to be vigilant in fighting it by making love. Once your honey has descended into a cortisol depression, you will think it is a good idea when the doctors give her serotonin enhancing drugs. Women in cortisol depressions can easily hurt themselves or others. I am not qualified enough to write about cortisol except as a scare tactic to make you take care of you honey and her serotonin depressions. Make love, don't take pills!

Nympho From Munich

A Newspaper Report

A woman dubbed the Nymphomaniac of Munich because of her insatiable sexual appetite has been found dead.

She was 47 years old, could not say 'nein' to men and would prowl the German city's bars in search of sex for pleasure partners. The curvy blonde twice hit the headlines for imprisoning lovers and forcing them to repeatedly have sex with her.

She lured men back to her apartment wearing skin-tight dresses revealing her ample bosom and drenched in perfume. One evening in April she met Mr. X and took him back to her flat where they had sex three times.

But that wasn't enough for her and when X tried to leave she locked the door and hid the keys. He told police she forced him to have sex another five times.

When she finally fell asleep he dashed to the balcony and called the cops. He told them: "You have got to help me. She is trying to kill me with sex. I cannot get out and I cannot go in."

When police smashed down the door to get in she begged the officers for a threesome. She was sent to a psychiatrist to be treated for sex addiction and told doctors she needed sex at least ten times a day every day.

The treatment failed and a few days later she left a secure hospital to catch a bus back home - and picked up a 31-year-old man on the way.

When they got back to the flat she hid his phone, locked the door and subjected him to a 36-hour sex ordeal. After he escaped he was found by passers-by naked and crying. He told them: "I met her on a bus. She invited me back here. Oh God, it was hell. I can't walk."

When police arrived she again invited them in for sex saying she wanted "a triple". She was sent back to a psychiatric unit and then released under the supervision of social workers but neighbors said they still saw her bringing back two or three men at the same time.

Her mother said her daughter was a tortured soul whose depression had triggered her obsession with sex.

Her husband had ditched her because he said she was too old and since then she had become obsessed with wanting to prove she was still attractive and sexy.

She had been a successful writer and owner of a fashion boutique but had seen her life destroyed when she became sex-crazed.

"My daughter was ill, a manic depressive. She was a victim of men," her mother said. She went on: "She only went wild when she had a manic phase."

However, the next night she was back in one of her favorite haunts, the Sunshine Bar in central Munich where she met a neighbor, a 31-year-old heating engineer called Mr. Y.

They went back to her flat where they downed a bottle of vodka and several bottles of wine while she snorted a white powder before they had sex several times.

They both fell asleep and when Y awoke the next morning he found her lifeless body next to him. He said: "I knew something was wrong because she usually wanted it first thing in the morning." An inquest this week heard that Y had tried to revive her after calling an ambulance.

German cops are waiting for the full post mortem but have ruled out foul play - they believe a cocktail of booze, drugs and sex caused her heart to stop.

Aphrodisiac Foods
To Increase Her Sexual Desire

Yes, I know. Viagra and its clones are the ultimate aphrodisiac. For men. While Viagra will help out women a little by making them more moist and their clitoris larger. *(Women get ED, erection dysfunction also, their clitoris's don't enlarge. No erection, no orgasm is the rule for women too.)* Women have been left out of the new sexual revolution Viagra has spawned. But not to worry. There are many foods that can make her so horny, she will tear your clothes off as soon as you enter the door. Interested? Read on, soon to be sexually sated male!

Celery. Yeah, right. I've seen this one before, it's a writer's imagination gone mad. Stop! It is true! Really! Here is why. Celery contains a chemical almost identical to the male pheromones, the odorless, tasteless chemical that women's bodies read. More than that, celery's chemical mimics the male's pheromone that pronounces that the man is ready to make love. The best way to utilize it is to eat celery together and stare into your girl's eyes as you do. Sometimes, just chop them together as you prepare dinner is the best way to get her to do 'it' on the kitchen table. *(Chopping releases more odors than slicing. Never chop onions, slice them)*

Cheese. Just to be fair in case any women are reading this, the smell of cheese increases erections in men. So if you are making love and he isn't quite as big as you might like, pop a piece of cheese in your mouth and blow in his nose as you kiss him!

Cucumber. This is a book on how to turn on women. So to be fair I have to mention that the smell of peeled and sliced cucumbers turns women on tremendously. Maybe that is why they eat those little cucumber sandwiches! For an added thrill, peel a medium cucumber and use it on her as a dildo. After make her eat it. It is hard to explain how turned on she will be. Get ready for the ride of your life! Women are complicated! Very!

Oysters. We all know that. Oysters contain zinc. Zinc is important for sperm production. Fine. But we are more interested in what influences the women. *(If any girls are reading this, check out my companion book: 'How to Turn your 60+ Man into a Red Hot Lover!')* The secret about oysters is they also contain dopamine, the hormone that makes women fall in love. When eating dopamine, a substance much like cocaine, be sure to touch her as she eats the oyster. She will fall in love with what is happening to her at the moment. Let her fall in love with your touch. WARNING! Dopamine works on you also. Be careful when you eat your oyster. You might fall in love with her too. Actually, wait a minute, what's wrong with that?

Watermelon. It's true! Who would have guessed. Watermelon contains citruline which relaxes the blood vessels feeding your sexual area, much like Viagra does. This works for both men and women. You get bigger, she gets softer and tighter! Plus it is fun to eat! It is best consumed on an empty stomach and without beer or spirits. Wine is OK. Try it! You'll love it! Spit out the seeds. I have it on good authority that white wine is better. *(But then my wife likes white wine anyway!)*

Honey. Forget sugar in your coffee. Sweeten it with honey instead. Actually, you can do anything you want to your coffee. Sweeten your girl's coffee with honey. Honey contains boron which metabolizes estrogen in your girl's blood stream. Estrogen is the hormone that makes your girl's vagina silky and tight. It doesn't do much for you, but who cares? Feed that girl honey!

Bananas. Sorry to have to break this to you if you really like bananas. They are great for women. Bananas create estrogen in humans. They turn your girl's vagina into paradise found. Much like honey, they tighten her vagina. However, bananas also create estrogen in males. If a man eats 5 large bananas in a row, he will have great difficulty attaining, and especially keeping, an erection. However he will be very loving and supportive. No doubt he will want to sip tea and talk about things with his girl. Sorry, guys, if you love bananas. You can always eat yours, after. One now and then is OK. When you go to dinner, make sure she gets the Banana Split for dessert and pour honey all over it!

Almonds. Sure almonds are good for you. Everyone knows that. But do you know that the smell of almonds make girls horny? They do and it works. Keep a couple of almonds in your pocket and munch on one before meeting with your girl. Sit close to her and watch her nipples harden and poke out inside of her bra. Even better if she doesn't wear a bra! Almonds don't do anything for men, but who cares? They do make him healthier but we are talking about sex here!

Chocolate. Sorry to have to tell you this. I know you have been religiously eating your dark chocolate. It isn't helping. The chocolate you need is unprocessed beans, called nibs. When they are cooked or pressed the chemical phenylethamine is destroyed. Phenylethamine is a tremendously powerful aphrodisiac for both sexes. Best thing to do, on your next vacation visit the tropics and find a cocoa bean farm. Stock up. The nibs don't have to be refrigerated. Maybe you are going to have to visit every year. No wonder people like Costa Rica so much! A handful will turn her incredibly on for about 4 hours. You better eat some too or she will wear you out!

Tofu. No, you don't have to eat it. Yes, it tastes yucky or at least it looks yucky. But it isn't for you. Soy products spike estrogen production in females. Estrogen is what gives her vagina that silky tight feeling. Hell, order some for both of you and have her eat both orders!

Avocados. If you are going to shack up with a nymphomaniac, you are going to need a lot of energy and stamina. Avocados contain more folic acid than any other food on the planet. Folic acid allows the body to metabolize protein to produce energy. It is the secret ingredient in all those health farms that are so popular. You can do it yourself. Eat an avocado for lunch, hell, eat two! Feed some to your girl too. After all, if you are going for a record, you don't want her to get tired on you!

Asparagus. There is sexual desire and libido. Libido is a general wanting to have sex and romance without a partner around. It is what makes you want to go out and find a partner. Sexual desire is when your body is aroused. Libido is in the mind, sexual desire in the body. Asparagus is called the Libido vegetable because of its high concentrations of vitamin E which turns on the mind, forces the mind to start thinking about sex.

Maca. This an ancient root grown in Peru high in the Andes that is dubbed a natural Viagra. It is sold in health food stores around the world, but unfortunately it only works when it is fresh and it isn't a supplement, it is a whole food. You have to eat a lot of it and it is very expensive in the health food stores. Oh, well!

Pumpkin Seeds. These seeds are rich in vitamins B, C, D, K, E and contain high levels of zinc, calcium and potassium. These are all good things for generating sperm. If you are going after nymphomaniacs you are going to need all the strength you can get!

Red Chilies. They are hot! Will they make you hot? Sorry, man. Chilies contain capsaicin which triggers the release of endorphins. Endorphins mimic morphine and opium in the human body. When your girl is really giving you a hard time because you had to stop after 24 times in 24 hours, eat some red chilies. They will make you feel cool, man. Real cool! Sorry, that was a chili joke. Chilies do shorten the refractory period, the time between orgasm and getting your next erection.

Garlic. Erections depend on getting good blood flow to the sexual organs. Unfortunately the arteries that feed the penis and the clitoris are the thinnest and narrowest in the human body. Garlic opens up these arteries letting the blood and the good times flow! If you eat them with parsley, your breath won't be as bad! Parsley is that little green thing you get with your steak and potato order.

Strawberries. These berries contain fenylethylamine which makes us fall in love. Fenylethylamine makes our palms sweat, eyes dilate, legs twitch, and heart pound when you kiss your sweetheart. It may not be true love, just a chemical reaction, but it sure feels like love! Is it good enough to keep your Honey on her Honeymoon for her entire life? Every night for the rest of her life?

Wheat Germ. It is tough to get enough vitamin E, the sex vitamin. Those vitamin tablets everyone takes don't really work. The body takes one look at those pills and says, 'This ain't food. Send it through to the end!' Get your vitamins in food. Sprinkle wheat germ on food instead of salt or pepper. It is a great taste as long as you don't over do it! Not only does it help in the sex department but it also helps in developing that six pack of muscles you have been trying for!

Red Wine. Red wine is good for everyone in moderation. It is very good for increasing testosterone production in women making them more aggressive in bed. Unfortunately it doesn't do anything for men, or more correctly, we already have so much testosterone we don't notice a bit more!

Coffee. Caffeine doesn't change you sexually but it does heighten her and your sensations. If sex with your girl is getting a bit passé, have a cup of coffee just before. You will be amazed at the difference!

Red Clover. I guess you could eat it, but mostly you make tea out of the flowers. No one knew about red clover until someone noticed that horse mares when grazing on red clover turned into nymphomaniacs. They jumped over fences to get to the stallions! Guess what? It works on humans too. The dried stuff you buy in little bags works OK. Find the newest bags they have. But for the real thing, pick your own. It isn't hard to find. It grows everywhere! Make tea or if you can talk her into it, have her eat the flowers! Wow! Make sure you are in shape first. It would be a bummer to have a heart attack when you are almost there on your tenth time!

Cinnamon. Sprinkle cinnamon onto food to keep your arteries in tip top shape but! BUT! Rub cinnamon on penises and clitorises. It is a wonderful, sexy sensation. Make love or just lick it off!

Nutmeg. Cinnamon is ok. Nutmeg has the same effect as cinnamon but you must realize that eating or absorbing the powder of three nutmegs is lethal. And there is no cure. If you want to play with nutmeg, do it very moderately!

Lose Weight Thru Sex

Look in any magazine or anywhere on the internet and you will find endless information about how sex will make a girl skinny. Included is info about how many calories she will burn in this position or that, and give the benefits of being on top instead of being on the bottom. The articles often come with soft porn pictures. Delicious reading, too bad they all have it completely wrong. She can lose weight by enjoying a full sex life, but not by performing in this position or that.

Losing weight is all about increasing muscles and increasing your metabolic rate. It doesn't matter how much you eat. If fact, often reducing your caloric intake will increase your weight over the long term. In the short term, yes you will lose weight as the body will burn off fat to make up for necessary energy. However, the first chance your body gets, it will pile that fat right back on again. This is because while dieting, you have been telling your body that food is scarce, hard to find. Your body is a finely tuned survival machine. If it thinks it has to, it will pile on the fat where ever it can all the while giving you so little energy for day to day operations that you are walking around tired and depressed. Diets don't work. Can you imagine a cave man on a diet? Ha! If the tribe managed to kill a mastodon, the whole tribe would sit around the fire and eat and eat and eat, make love, fall asleep and then eat and love some more. Some how his cave didn't come equipped with a deep freezer. They had to eat before their windfall started to rot. During those eons so long ago, our genetic code was developed. One of the most interesting part of that code is the combination of eating, exercise and making love doesn't make you fat. In fact, if a girl orgasms three times a day with a guy, she will never get fat. *(Sorry, sorry. Lesbians really get ripped off here. Most of the reason this works is the hormones the man releases into the woman's vagina when he ejaculates, alters the woman's metabolic rate for an hour or two. If he ejaculated into her three times a day, the effect last all day long.)*

When a man ejaculates, yes sperm is released, but also the seminal fluid created mostly by the prostate gland to give the sperm something to swim in and to alter the fluids in the vagina into a sperm friendly environment. This fluid also contains significant amounts of the following hormones: testosterone, adrenaline and vasopressin. These hormones influence the woman to have more sex. If her current partner has fallen asleep, she will wander around the cave until she finds another part time lover. Biologically, her body is seeking a wide variety of sperm in hopes the best of all will make it to the egg first. The testosterone makes the woman more aggressive in seeking more loving. The adrenaline keeps her from going to sleep no matter how much her current lover is yawning. The vasopressin is interesting. It keeps people monogamous. So if she really likes her current lover, she will pinch and shove him until he wakes up and gets down to business.

It doesn't matter which way you make love. If the girl goes down on you, tell her to hold your ejaculate in her mouth as long as she can. Swallowed into the stomach, the hormones are destroyed. In the mouth, the hormones are absorbed by the semi-permeable membranes under the tongue. Tell her it will make her skinny and she will swirl it around eagerly!

Guys, tough luck. You aren't going to get skinnier by more sex. But wait. Having more sex does mean that you aren't going to be swilling beer in front of the TV as much, it means you aren't going to be shoving your mouth full of chips and pretzels. Yes, sex will make you skinnier too!

Mystery Woman #2
Estrogen Addict
From a Sailing Doctor's ER Files

"Any patient whose symptoms involve nausea and vomiting are the last called in the ER. No one wants their examination room contaminated on a busy shift. I almost didn't take her but I had a few minutes between gun shots and stabbings so I grabbed her file and nodded for her to come in.

"What have you been taking that is making you upchuck?" She didn't respond but dug in her bag, it was too big to be called a purse, and pulled out a packet of oral estrogen pills.

"How many are you taking?" Estrogen pills are for older women going through menopause. She looked to be 21 or 22 and as healthy as could be.

"It varies. I don't keep track. At least one an hour, I guess." I looked closely at her eyes. She wasn't hallucinating.

"Why do you take so many? They will make you sick. No wonder you are upchucking."

"To make money. The estrogen makes my pussy more luscious. Men will pay serious money for a pussy like mine. And once they have me, they are hooked. You must know what estrogen does to a pussy, don't you?"

"It makes your vagina thicker and softer."

"Yeah. These men, they say they love me, bull, they love it! They will pay anything to get more of it. That is why I am here. I have a really rich client coming by tonight. He is really loaded. So I took a whole bottle of estrogen. Then I started throwing up. How can I take them without vomiting?"

"You know that much estrogen will eventually kill you? Hormones are really powerful. You can really screw yourself up."

"I know. But I want to make a million before I'm 30. Then I'll give it up. It's tough being poor. I hate it. I'd rather be sick. It's a trade off. So, can you help me or what?"

(Doctor's Name withheld by request.)

Your Astrological Sign and Sex

I was educated in the sciences and have a difficult time reading about astrology without laughing, however, having been educated in the sciences, when I look at the data it is obvious that astrology in some weird way correlates to reality. People really do seem to behave differently depending on the day of the year that they are born. Weird but true. Part of turning your woman into a raving nymphomaniac is to pick the right woman for you. To make sure the right chemistry is there from the start. If it turns out that your one and only isn't as compatible as you originally thought, then at least you know you are in for an uphill battle and won't be upset at early set backs. This is the best information I can find, logic says it is imaginary, experience says it works. Your choice!

Aries

People born under this sign mature sexually early in life. They are aroused easily and orgasm quickly. If you are a man, try to stay physically fit and active to be able to prolong your love making to please your partner. Women born under this sign tend to like to make love in unusual locations. If she was born between noon and 4 PM she is a very sexual being and has potential to become a nymphomaniac.

Taurus

People born under this sign are very sensuous and seek to enjoy a full sexual life. Men need to dress well and keep in shape to maximize their sexuality. They normally can stay active their entire life. Taurus women love beauty as their ruling planet is Venus, the Goddess of Physical Beauty. When they wear perfumes, they become even more sexual. If she was born between 10 AM and 2 PM and has a comfortable life style, she is very likely to be able to become a nymphomaniac.

Gemini

People born under this sign become easily bored with routine in their sex life. Men are in danger of becoming involved with too many different women and burning themselves out early in life. Women are almost incapable of obtaining orgasm in the same position twice in a row. Of all the signs, Gemini women are the most likely to enjoy a threesome in bed, especially in the third is another woman. If she was born between 8 AM and noon, she has potential to become a nymphomaniac. However, realize she will want to do it in different ways, in different places and with different music in the background each time she makes love.

Cancer

If you want a woman that will stay married to you all your life and never even look at another man, a Cancer girl is your best bet. She is unlikely to be able to orgasm outside of her own home and she only becomes sexual when she is happy with herself and is sure of your love for her. She will tend to live in the past but if she was born between 6am and 10am and you can keep her away from the past, she has every potential to become a nymphomaniac at least one night a month.

Leo

People born under this sign are party animals. They like to have a good time and enjoy themselves. Leo men normally become active early as do Leo women. She will become more sexual if you take her out on the town and tell her jokes. To get her to make love more than once in a night be prepared to offer her some other kind of amusement between orgasms. If she was born between 4am and 8am and if you can keep her amused and laughing, she has every potential to become a nymphomaniac.

Virgo

Virgos are intensely sexual creatures but refuse to admit it to themselves. She approaches sex in a, "but we already did it last night!" manner. However, inside she is a sexual volcano. The only problem is how to get all that red hot lava out into the open where she is willing to talk about it. Maybe even do some of it! If she was born between 2am and 6am she might be willing to adventure out of her secret cave. If you can, you might have one of the most powerful of the nymphomaniacs in our astrological world!

Libra

People born under this sign feel they have to spend a lot of time deciding whether or not to have sex, how to have sex, when to have sex and who to have sex with. Once she makes up her mind, she is unlikely to change it. If she was born between midnight and 4am and decides that she is going to do an all nighter with you, you are going to understand the true spirit of a nymphomaniac!

Scorpio

People born under this sign are the most sexual of all. 45% of all nymphomaniacs are Scorpios. She will take charge in bed if you aren't doing it to her satisfaction and if she didn't get off properly, she will make you do it over and over until you get it right! She will always be true to herself, she is not one who will fake an orgasm. If she was born between the hours of 10pm and 2am and she decides to take you to bed, hang on to her if you can! She is the most sexual creature you are ever likely to meet! You will definitely remember her for the rest of your life! If you can, hang on to her, if you can keep up!

Sagittarius

People born under this sign tend to be long distance lovers. When you say goodbye to a lover who is moving to a new city, a Sagittarius girl writes every week; for years. As such, her sex life tends to be erratic, a feast or famine experience. If she was born between 8pm and midnight and you moved away and then moved back, you are going to go for the record. She will screw your brains out and won't stop till she loses control of her legs. Just be aware that for her, writing a letter is a form of foreplay.

Capricorn

People born under this sign like to say, "Everything in Moderation." Yes, that means sex, too. She is very conservative in bed and is not easily or quickly brought to orgasm. If she was born between the hours of 6pm and 10pm and you manage to get her motor up to speed, she will keep going all night long. At least for what is left of the night!

Aquarius

People born under this sign are more likely to become thinkers and planners than doers. She can be talked into having sex, if the argument is logical. She is the most likely of the signs to be a lesbian. Being a lesbian is logical. No mess, no children! She does like variety in sex and if she was born between 4pm and 8pm it would not be that difficult to talk her into having on orgy or at least a threesome, the sex of the third, not important!

Pisces

People born under this sign would make great spies except they usually don't like to make love unless they are desperately in love first. She likes to make up stories of what you do out of her sight, always of some important job you are doing to help save the world. It doesn't seem to matter if the stories have any relation to the truth. If she was born between 2 pm and 6 pm she will like to sneak around and have sex in secret spots. Strange buildings and deep forests are her favorite locals. I hope you were a boy scout!

Are your star signs a valid way to find a sexually active women? Are all Scorpios raving nymphomaniacs? If they believe they are, then they are that much closer to being one!

Decreasing Your Refractory Period

The refractory period is the amount of time between your orgasm and your next erection. Women have a refractory period also but theirs lasts a few minutes at the most. Women were born to be nymphomaniacs. Physically, they can make love all night long. Men on the other hand, may have to wait up to an hour for their next erection. The younger you are, the shorter the period you need to rest. It would be a sad thing indeed to turn your girl into a nymphomaniac and not be able to anything about it! Take heart! You can decrease your refractory period! You can make love all night long!

Oxytocin is the hormone that causes erections in men *(and clitoral erections in women)*. To maintain an erection a steady supply of oxytocin must be present. Oxytocin also shortens the refractory period between male erections. The release of oxytocin by the body can be controlled by the mind.

Oxytocin is the love hormone. When you stare into your girls eyes *(and her into yours)* oxytocin is released. This a biochemical defense for a monogamous marriage. The longer you stay married, as long as you make love and both parties orgasm *at least* 3 times a week, the stronger the release of oxytocin will be. The trick is to make love, come together if you can, hold on to each other for the five minute refractory period *she* needs, then stare into her eyes *(without laughing, please!)* and kiss her passionately. If this doesn't work the first couple times you try it, you have to train your body to release oxytocin on command.

The next time you both are feeling frisky, plan for a prolonged foreplay. Invent a cue for your body. I like staring into each other's eyes but it can be anything. Kissing each other's necks, playing with each other's nipples, *(a lightly pinched nipple, either sex, naturally releases oxytocin)* or just hold hands. In any case, do your cue as you tease each other to arousal. Do this every time you make love. Be consistent.   After a surprisingly short time your body will learn to release oxytocin on the performance of your cue.

The nipples of either sex are great releasers or oxytocin. Like the clitoris they should be teased to arousal by a very light touch with a finger tip or tongue tip at first. After the nipple swells in response, a light flick of a finger nail or a light momentary pinch between fingers will cause the nipple to become erect and harden the surrounding areole.   The penis *(or clitoris)* is by now mostly erect.

I know that the philosophy of sadism/masochism is frowned upon in today's culture *(in contrast to France in the 1800's)* but some of their techniques do work on all human bodies. Pain applied to the human nipple will increase erection size, sometimes dramatically. The trick is to make the pain momentary. Pain applied for long periods *(as suggested by s/m adherents)* only hardens the nipples and reduces the effect. So, pinch, lick, suck, bite the nipples, but just for a second or two. Wait for five or ten seconds and do it again. The results are astounding.

If your penis still isn't responding, have your girl play with your anus. Did I just say that in print. Yes, I did. It does work. The anus has a plethora of nerve endings and a major nerve leads directly to the penis. She can slip a finger just inside the anus however care must be taken not to go too far in or to push a penis sized object into the colon. This will cause an immediate deflation of the penis. *(Unless one is of the homosexual persuasion.)*

More on this subject can be found in this book's female companion, *"How to Turn Your 60+ Man in to a Red Hot Lover. For Women Only."* Written, of course, by Me! Look for it on Kindle.

Mystery Woman #3

Tied up in the Seychelles
A True Story

I was single handing my Columbia Challenger 24' sailboat in those days. I would take crew once in a while, put it was fun in those long ago days before the AIDS epidemic to sail alone and in each new port discover the joys of the universal female desire to have sex with a man, repeatedly, and then to have him leave never to return. Too often, women become involved with a guy and after, they can't get rid of him! Sometimes, a girl just wants a roll in the hay, not a lifetime of devotion/stalking.

I met Mystery Woman #3 in the Seychelles boat sitting a nice ketch anchored next to me. Let's call her Virginia (not her real name). She was into sadism. She liked to hurt as she made love. Especially my nipples. She pinched them, she bit them, she poured hot wax on them. I would have left instantly except I had foolishly let her tie me up first, and she was very good with knots!

I was astonished that my penis responded to her tortures. She wouldn't make love to me until she had increased by penis size by 50% bigger than it had ever been in by life. After I came I wasn't allowed a moments rest. She was at me again. Biting, sucking with a vacuum, dabbing with hot sauce. *(The hot wax wasn't as bad as the first time when the cooled wax tore all my chest hair out!)*

I learned a lot from her. I learned I really didn't like being tied up, at least not by a woman I didn't know. I learned that the human body is a lot more complicated than what we were taught in Sex Ed. I learned that light pain can be a tremendous turn on in sex. I learned to watch out for single women living on a ketch, if they invite you aboard, and watch out for ropes!

Sex During Menopause

Yes, no problem. You can have sex after and during menopause. In fact, sex during menopause will help your girl get through the change. There is a lot of information out there that isn't correct, mostly because there are 12 different types of menopause each with different symptoms. Study this chapter well and figure out which type your girl has, then follow the guidelines for that type of menopause. I hope your lady has an easy time of it.

Type 1. The Ideal Menopause
Ideal as the girl has few if any symptoms or discomfort. It is all over in 12 to 15 months. If your girl has type 1, go out and buy a lottery ticket. You are one lucky guy, or rather your girl is one hell of a lucky woman! You don't need to do anything except fall on your knees each night and thank whatever gods there may be for this blessing!

Type 2. Low Testosterone
Low because her body is making either no or not enough testosterone. She will feel a lack in confidence and a loss of 'vim and vigor.' She might have a mild depression but will likely still be interested in sex as long as you start the ball rolling. The worse symptom for her is a loss of skin tone. Her body and especially her face will develop wrinkles. If she is producing almost no testosterone her labia and vulva will become thin and fragile making sex more painful for her. Be sure to stock up on personal lubricant. If your girl has low testosterone, there are skin patches she can stick on, however it works just as well to have oral sex. Seminal fluid, released with the sperm, contains large amounts of testosterone however if she swallows, the stomach acids destroy the hormone, so it is better for her to hold the ejaculate in her mouth and swish it around. She may refuse at first because she will feel it is just too yucky, however if she tries it and her face starts to lose her wrinkles, she will be a convert. If you have had a vasectomy, no problem. The seminal fluid remains the same.

Type 3. High Testosterone
Like Type 2, estrogen and progesterone are at normal levels, so symptoms are likely to be mild. The most pronounced are that she will feel angry and agitated. She will likely develop facial hair, acne and oily skin. However, high testosterone in women often causes adult onset diabetes. To combat that, be sure she doesn't eat candy to help with her anger. She will get angry when she wants sex. Get in the habit of reaching between her legs and massaging her, her high testosterone will love it.

Type 4. Low Estrogen
Here come the hot flashes! That isn't a joke. Nor is low estrogen which decreases her verbal skills; especially she will have trouble remembering even close friend's names. Plus her manual dexterity will decrease, making sewing and other fine motor tasks difficult. However the worse is stress incontinence (wetting her pants when she sneezes or coughs) and/or excessive vaginal bleeding, reduction in breast size and thinner skin. All in all not a good menopause. Health wise, estrogen regulates bone density so Type 4 increases the risk for osteoporosis and estrogen also protects women against heart attacks. A lack of estrogen opens her up to cardiac problems and many forms of cancer. Be as sweet and loving as loving as you can be. Start going to church. Those monks could go years without sex. *(Reportedly!)*

Type 5. Low Estrogen, Low Testosterone
This is a double whammy. She will have many of the effects of types 2 and 4 however the worse symptom is devastating depression, you will swear that she doesn't love you anymore. She will have trouble learning new things, not that she wants to anyway. It doesn't help her mood that her breasts will sag almost overnight and she will develop wrinkles over most of her body. She will not help during sex. She will likely just lay there. Keep telling her how beautiful she is, how sexy she makes you feel. Depression is a terrible thing.

Type 6. Low Estrogen, High Testosterone
This type doesn't sound as bad but it is. She will experience increased agitation and higher fatigue but she will be unable to

sleep making her even more tired and irritable. She will want sex, due to her high testosterone but the sexual act will be too painful for her. Maybe the worse for her is her hair will thin dramatically, in some cases leading to baldness. If she is adventurous, introduce her to anal sex. Some kind of sex will make her feel much better.

Type 7. Low Progesterone
Progesterone protects your girl's nervous system. She will suffer very high anxiety in this type of menopause. Her body is suffering a withdrawal from progesterone and will act like it is having a withdrawal from heroin. She will wake up in the middle of the night screaming in fear, have very vivid, scary dreams and still be sure every night that there is a prowler in the house. Progesterone also protects the body from pain and inflammation and low levels increase the chance for osteoporosis. She will be as interested in sex as she always was, except her desire to cuddle will disappear with her progesterone.

Type 8. Low Progesterone, Low Testosterone
The symptoms in this type are the same as type 7 but added to it is no will power to do anything about the symptoms or with her life. Sex is of no interest, and even if she agrees to do it, she is so achy she can't enjoy it. She will still have the nightmares but will lack the energy to scream and will just lay in bed crying.

Type 9. Low Progesterone, High Testosterone
Poor girl has the anxiety of low progesterone and the anger and testiness of high testosterone. She will over react to everything. Little mole hills become the Alps in mere seconds. Not only sleep is a problem, but if she can nod off, she suffers from sleep apnea. *(When you stop breathing during sleep and then start again with a big gasp.)* She will want sex but if anything is not right, if it takes too long, she will blame you.

Type 10. Low Estrogen, Low Progesterone
You are going to have a sad little puppy of a girl with this one. She will be depressed, feel hopelessness in the face of the smallest problem and futility at her ability to solve any of them not that it matters because she won't be able to remember what happened

yesterday clearly. Of all the types, in this one she will have the most trouble with wetting her pants Like type 7 she will seem like she is withdrawing from heroin and like type 4 she will lose the ability to do fine work with her hands.   All in all, she is likely to be a suicide risk except she doesn't have the determination. Try to be as nice as you can be to her. Your honey will come back to you in a couple of years. You did say for better or worse didn't you? Well this is definitely, the worse. Might as well forget about sex. It isn't worth the trouble.

Type 11. Low Estrogen, Low Progesterone, Low Testosterone
This one is the bottom of the pit. You are not going to be able to handle her yourself. You are going to need help. Hopefully you have family and friends around to take her off your hands once in a while. Sex is history. Even if you could get her to try, it will be so painful that she will scream in pain and horror for the whole time and for days afterwards. You definitely must think about getting hormone replacement tablets.   If not after she gets through menopause, she might have damaged herself emotionally and mentally—you might not get your Honey back, she will be a stranger. Get help. Not for her, for you. You are going to need counseling.

Type 12. Low Estrogen, Low Progesterone, High Testosterone
This type of menopause is much like the last except she is able to scream in frustration. The screams might be hard for you but they give her a release. Type 12 always develop insulin resistance and almost always develop diabetes. She will have to be treated for this or her life expectancy will decrease by decades. You will have to give her the shots. She won't be able to do them herself. She will want sex, she will scream that she wants you to screw her, but if you do the pain will be so high, she will scream that you are killing her. Best thing to do is forget about sex and get counseling for the two of you. Separately. This is a tough one, but at least when it is over, your honey will eventually recover. Start getting fit for a halo. You are going to earn it.

Sex After Menopause

Take a big sigh of relief. Both of you got through menopause and you still love each other. Well, almost. If she went through type 8 to 12, you are going to have to rebuild your love. It will have mostly self destructed during menopause. But, with luck, the same girl you married will return to you to enjoy your sunset years together.

Sex after menopause is wonderful. No more worry about getting pregnant, no more yucky birth control pills to take. The kids have mostly gone off, his and maybe her retirement is kicking in. It is time to take long holidays, take that cruise you always wanted, now you have time to read as many books as you want. True the sex isn't filled with fireworks anymore. It is more genteel, more of an act of love rather than desire. Now is the time to cuddle with each other, now is the time that the love you have always had for each other finally comes to bloom. She is sexually more active, he is slowing down. Chances are that now is the time that they will orgasm together, finally!

There are problems. She will often find her vagina dry no matter how turned on she is. Be kind and be gentle. On the fold of skin that hides the clitoris are two little spots that when rubbed will increase her lubrication. (For detailed information, read my book, *'How to Turn Your 60+ Man into a Red Hot Lover, For Women Only.'* Available on Kindle and as always on board the Good Ship, Beau Soleil!

As we age, sex becomes less intense. Your legs won't tremble at the touch of your girl, her vagina won't become wet at the thought of you. Not to worry. The key is foreplay. And now you have the time. Just remember, foreplay for her starts with her doing something for you, cooking you a meal, making your bed. If you can convince her that you really truly want her sexually because she is the most fantastic girl in the world for you, the battle is won. Foreplay for you is buying her something. It doesn't have to be candy or flowers. Your testosterone will increase just by buying her something.

But forget the problems. There are more joys than problems. The first and foremost joy is your honey is now going to turn into a nymphomaniac if she ever is going to. Women undergo a genesis after menopause that rekindles their desire for sex. Not only for sex, but for repeated sex, all night long.

The kids are gone, if she worked, demands at work are easing or she might have already quit. Social Security payments are finally coming in, supplying an added sense of 'all is right with my world.' She can see the end of the rainbow up ahead and she is wondering what is on the other side. She has time to read those steamy romance novels and finds herself turned on easier than when she was younger. Life is good! Finally!

She will soon learn that just going through the actions of loving her man that she performed for years earlier, singing while cooking, gently lifting her man's legs while she vacuums under them, etc will bring back those old feelings of romance. Just as hormones can encourage us to behave in certain ways, behaving in certain ways after years of experience will evoke the hormones to cascade. Kissing her man passionately, even though she doesn't feel any passion, will cause a cascade and in a remarkably short time, often only seconds, her passion will flow. Equally well, this works on men. If your organ is just sitting there flaccid, playing with her body will resurrect it within seconds. The only trick is, don't pretend. Get into it heart and soul. There is no reason that the two of you can't be orgasmic well into your 90's and even beyond.

She can sense the end coming a couple of decades ahead and she starts to worry that she might die and her dance card will still have empty spaces inside. It is time to start experiencing what she has been putting off for all these years. Foremost in every woman's mind, is exploring sex to its fullest extent. Suddenly, she wants to make love all night long. She wants to go around the world, at least once. If you are her lucky guy, hold on to your hat! Your life is just about to get way more interesting! Hallelujah! God be praised!

Her passion will awaken yours from where it hid during the long years of menopause, especially if she had a tough time of it. You married her for better or worse. You got through the worse, guess what? You thought that the love making was better on your honeymoon? It wasn't. The best is loving each other into the sunset. That is love. That is glory. That is what we were designed for. Making love over and over, each night and for every night of our lives!

Afterword

In the interests of full disclosure, I must be the first to tell you that my wife and editor of some 26 years still insists that she is not a nymphomaniac even though her zodiac sign assigns her that ranking, barely by 3 minutes. But then she is a Virgo so she wouldn't admit it anyway!

But there is hope for her yet! I've never met anyone like her. We orgasm together almost every time we make love. Maybe we were made for each other?

Women are what make life worth while. Treasure them, love them, please them; and make love to them every time you can. That is the secret of a happy life. If your hormones are happy, you will be happy. Really, it is that simple! Who knew?

www.ingramcontent.com/pod-product-compliance
Lightning Source LLC
Chambersburg PA
CBHW071853020426
42331CB00007B/1983